Guitar Images

MB22193

by William Bay

I0804501

A double cd recording containing the author's performance of each solo is available from Mel Bay Publications. (www.melbay.com) The product number for the double cd package is #11142CD

BILL'S MUSIC SHELF

Visit us on the Web at www.melbay.com or www.billsmusicshelf.com

Contents

Preface

The solos in this collection present a myriad of moods on the guitar. I wrote them to be very expressive, contemplative pieces which could be performed in a variety of secular and sacred settings. Most of them are from three solo collections I previously authored entitled "Guitar Meditations" (MB22029), "Guitar Airs and Ballads" (MB22039) and "Timeless Solos for Guitar" (MB22041). Some of the pieces were scored for 7 string guitar; however, they can be performed quite successfully on 6 string guitar. I have indicated the alternate 6 string pedal tones in the tablature part. I included tablature because many of the solos use a "cross-picking" technique alternating higher position closed strings and open strings, resulting in a "harp-like" effect. I find that tablature gives an easy way to show this and clarifies where these passages should be played on the fingerboard. I also used Dropped D tuning on a number of the pieces. I love the rich resonance that tuning gives the instrument.

I would like to say a word about the pieces taken from "Timeless Solos". These solos contain no time signatures or bar lines. I did this because I wanted the solos to be very expressive in interpretation yet "free-form" in structure. The companion recording presents my interpretation of these works. You may interpret them differently and that is fine! When writing these solos I first envisioned the form as an extended "cadenza". However, from my earlier trumpet playing days I recalled that, especially in the 19th century, a cadenza was a momentary break in a solo which gave the performer a chance to dazzle the audience with his or her virtuosity. These solos are not about that. Rather, they are a vehicle written to give the guitarist an opportunity to move the listener with the performer's expressive ability. I also thought of these solos in the form of a "chant". However, most chants are monophonic in form and these solos in various parts present a fairly lush harmonic structure.

All of these solos may be performed by the classical or fingerstyle guitarist or, as I perform them, with a pick. I hope you explore the diverse moods presented in this collection and make full use of the many avenues of expression offered in these pieces.

William Bay

Light Through Mist

I want to say a few things about the first solo presented, "Light Through Mist" This is one of my favorites. I was in Sydney, Australia recently and visited the Museum of Contemporary Art. There was a special exhibit by Danish artist, Olafur Eliasson. One of his exhibits was called "Beauty". To enter this exhibit you walked through a long dark tunnel and then entered a room where the floor, walls and ceiling were painted black. There were no windows in the room and the only light was a tiny, mini-flood light on the ceiling in the far corner of the room. This floodlight was directed on a very fine water vapor mist descending from the ceiling. It was a captivating experience. You could feel the moisture in the room and smell the water vapor. As you the mist descended from the ceiling, it continually changed shape. A different pattern of light and mist appeared each second. I found this to be a very ethereal, enchanting yet somewhat eerie experience. I decided to write a piece of music capturing the mystical feeling of this exhibit and "Light Through Mist" is what I came up with. I hope you enjoy it!

Light Through Mist

⑦ = A

Andante ♩ = 90

William Bay

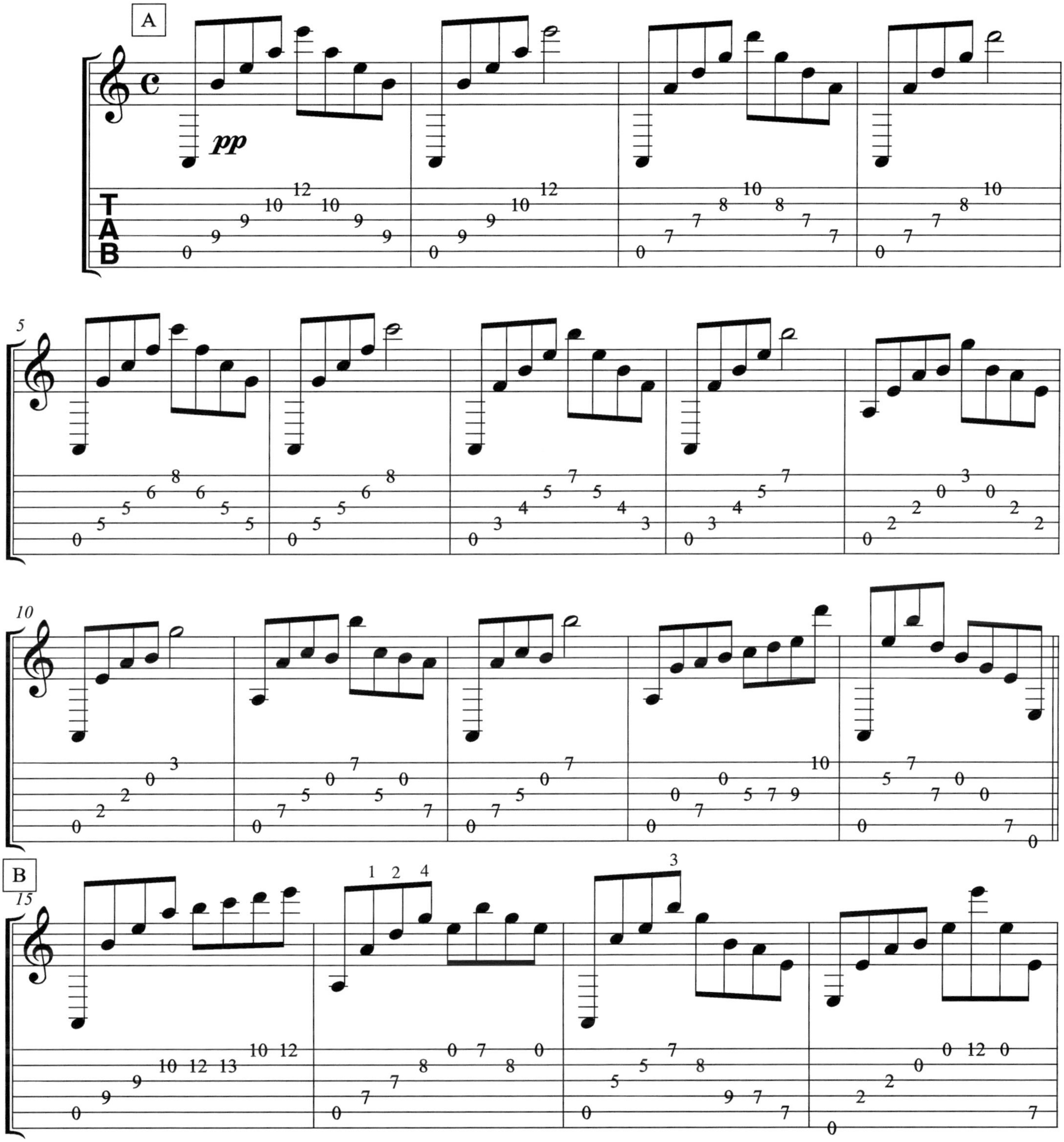

C
D
E

44
49
F
54
59
64
rit.

Peace

⑦ = A

Dropped D Tuning

Adagio ♩ = 72

William Bay

C
2
D
p

mf
E
mf
mp
p
pp
ppp
pppp

Regret

⑦ = B

Largo ♩ = 55

William Bay

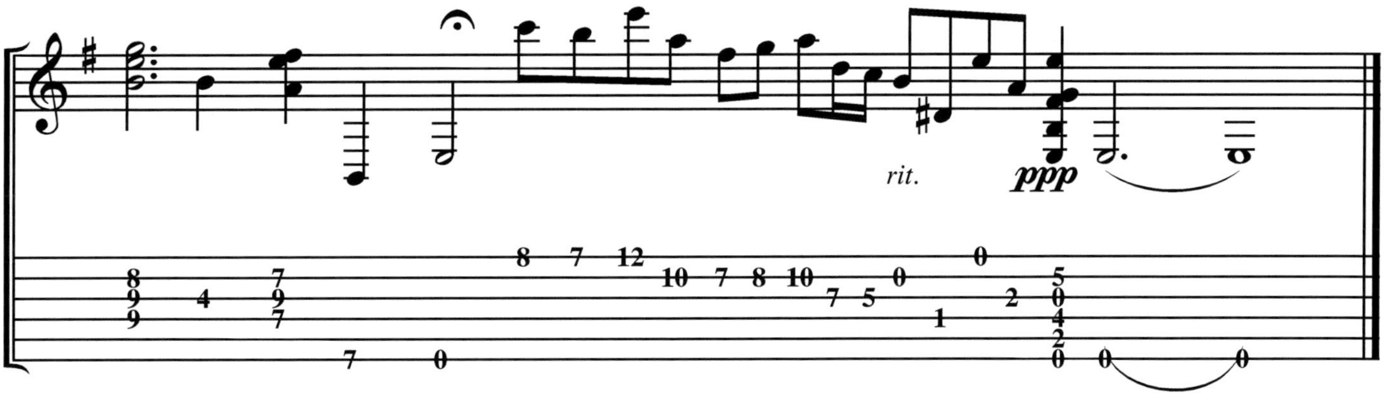
rit.
ppp

New Day

⑦ = A

William Bay

Andante ♩ = 80

C
D
22
28
34
39
44

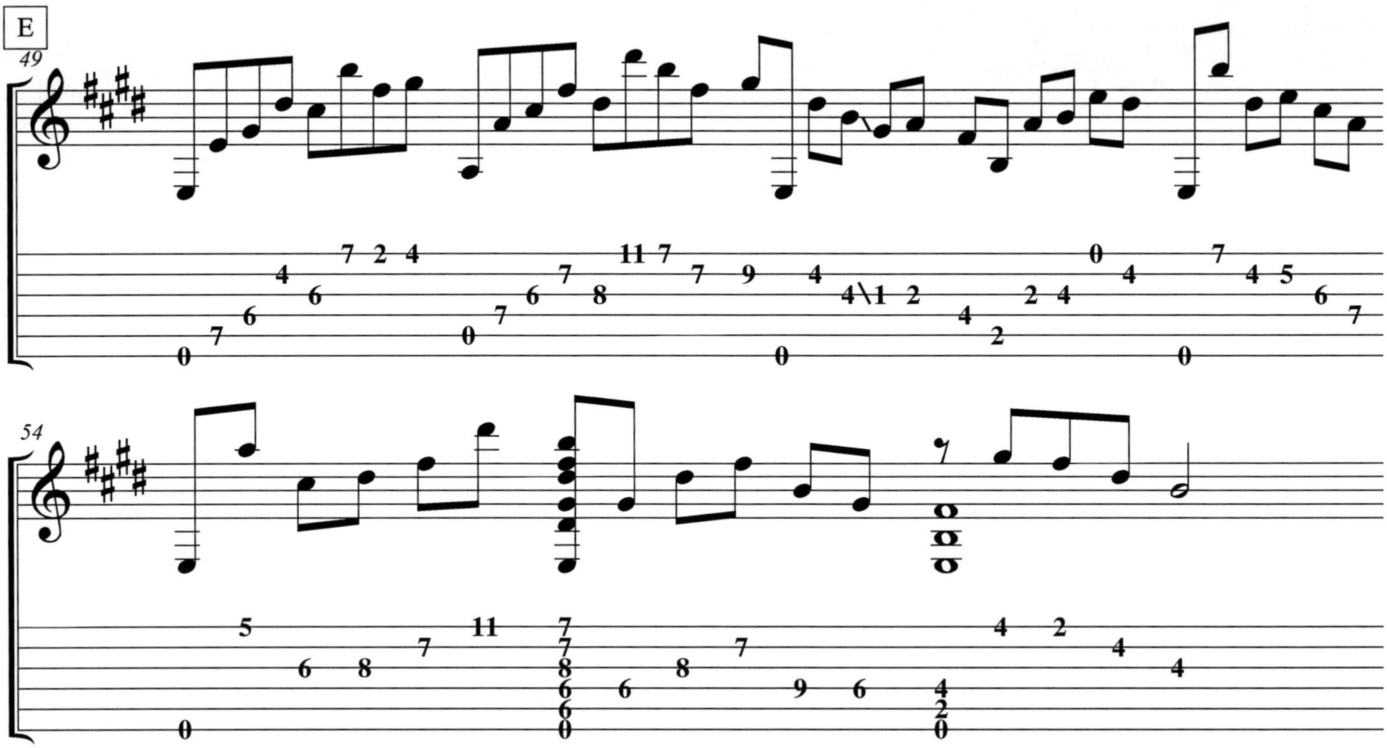
E
49
54

This page has been left blank
to avoid awkward page turns.

Longing

⑦ = A

William Bay

Adagio ♩ = 66

19
24
30
36
42
mf
p
pp

Hope

William Bay

This page has been left blank
to avoid awkward page turns.

Horizon

⑦ = A

Freely

William Bay

mf
p
pp
f
p
mp
p
pp

Assurance

Adagio ♩= 72

Dropped D Tuning

William Bay

D

Distant Homeland

⑦ = A

William Bay

16
p
mf
20
24
rit.
ppp

Vigil

⑦ = A

Slowly, With Feeling ♩ = 68

William Bay

25
30
35
39
43

47
52
58
65

Morning Aire

Dropped D Tuning

⑥ = D
⑦ = A

William Bay

rit.

Alone

⑦ = B

William Bay

Very Slowly ♩ = 70

38
42
46
rit.
50
54
rit.
Harm. 12th Fret
ppp

This page has been left blank
to avoid awkward page turns.

A Place of Rest

⑦ = B

William Bay

Slowly, with feeling

mp
Slowly, a tempo
mp
Harm 12
rit.

Clouds

Dropped D Tuning

William Bay

Slowly, With Feeling ♩ = 70

37
rit.
41
rall.
44
mp
p
rit.
pp

Gentle Voice

⑦ = A

William Bay

16
19
23
27
31

35
38
41
rit.
pp

Sleeping Child

William Bay

46
51
56
61
mp
p
rit.
pp

Daydreams

Dropped D Tuning

⑥= D

William Bay

Slowly, With Expression

rall.
a tempo
p
pp

Reverie
Dropped D Tuning

⑥ = D

William Bay

17
Slower
21
25
a tempo
29
33
Slower

a tempo
Boldly

58
62
67
rit.
pp

The Sea of Recollection

Dropped D Tuning

⑥= D

William Bay

H
P
TAB

Prairie Sunrise

William Bay

P
Harm.

This page has been left blank
to avoid awkward page turns.

Fields of Culloden

Dropped D Tuning

⑥ = D

⑦ = A

William Bay

mp
f
sl.
P

rit.

39
f
42
p
45
mf
47
p
rit.
ppp

Sweet Memories

⑦= A

William Bay

This page has been left blank
to avoid awkward page turns.

Charlie's Lament

Dropped D Tuning

(6) = D

(7) = A

William Bay

Slowly, With Feeling ♩ = 68

C
D
mf
E
mp

F
G
rit.

H
rit.
I

Morning Carol

Dropped D Tuning

⑥ = D
⑦ = A

William Bay

Moderately, with expression

14
18
21
24
pp

My Irish Home

Dropped D Tuning

⑥ = D

⑦ = A

William Bay

Larghetto ♩ = 64

rit.
pp